De

BY

Will Hanafin

Published in 2001 by
Merlin Publishing
16 Upper Pembroke Street
Dublin 2
Ireland
www.merlin-publishing.com

ISBN 1-903582-10-5

Hanafin, Will
De Little Book of Bertie
1. Ahern, Bertie, 1951-
2. Prime ministers – Ireland
I. Title
941.7'0824'092

Typeset by Gough Typesetting Services, Dublin
Printed by Colour Books Ltd, Dublin

Contents

Bertie-isms

DUCK!

"I don't think it helps people to start throwing white elephants and red herrings at each other."

Questions and Answers • RTÉ • 28 March 1994

DON'T ASK ME!

"My own personal position is irrelevant in this."

(Going into coalition with Labour)

Farrell • RTÉ • 20 November 1994

PICK OF THE CROP

"And you can't find money on trees."

Questions and Answers • RTÉ • 28 March 1994

NOTHIN' PERSONAL, LIKE

"It's no point in personalising any of the people involved in this."

Questions and Answers • RTÉ • 7 December 1992

BAD ROLE MODELS?

*"I'd go and buy meself a country home or an
offshore island or something like that."*

(On winning the Lottery)

RTÉ News • 22 March 1987

BENEFIT OF THE DOUBT?

"Armed both with revolvers, pistols and baseball bats, and I suppose we could all conclude that, whatever they were about, they were up to no good."

(Talking about Real IRA arrests)

Oireachtas Report • RTÉ • 31 January 2001

OPPOSITION OPTIONS

"Now we will be an aggressive Opposition where we oppose things and we'll support things that we support."

RTÉ News • 26 September 1995

STATING THE OBVIOUS

"Every party knows that the composition of the next government will be determined by the electorate."

Sunday Independent • 31 December 2000

POLL POSITION

"I think every opinion poll is just a snapshot of events at any particular time."

The Irish Times • 21 November 2000

HUMBLE PIE

"(They)... are trying to upset the apple tart."

The Irish Times Magazine • 19 May 2001

ALL THE WORLD'S
A STAGE

*"You only have one life.
This isn't a rehearsal."*

The Late Late Show • RTÉ • 25 May 2001

TERMINATOR TOO

"The grass roots, or the rank and file, are now made from fibre-optics."

The Irish Times • 7 March 1995

INDIGESTION

"We all have to swallow humble pie, and I have been doing it for years, but if you keep at it, you can break through and get selected at the convention."

The Irish Times • 21 November 1994

MAN OF THE PEOPLE

"... I came up through the people system."

The Irish Times • 5 June 1997

DIRT TRIBUNAL

*"Let's put the dirty linen, the clean linen on
the table — deal with them —
Take the recommendations..."*

Later with O'Leary • RTÉ • 31 May 2000

TEMPORARY CEASEFIRE

"Those groups who are not on ceasefire or even maybe those who are on ceasefire at the edges might be involved in some activities."

(at the Fianna Fáil Ard-Fheis),

RTÉ News • 4 March 2000

URBAN GUERRILLAS

"Charles J. Haughey wanted to transform Temple Bar into Ireland's West Bank."

The Irish Times Magazine • 19 May 2001

BETTER THAN SEX

*"If I can help in getting a person a house
or a medical card, it is as good as scoring
a goal on Sunday."*

Sunday Press • 24 February 1983

LIMBO DANCING

"In political life, you have a hassle period of some difficulties. I'm neither separated nor totally the best family man in the world. I'm in between."

In Dublin • 10 April 1991

TIME TRAVELLERS

"There's one thing I can't do...
I can't change the past..."

RTÉ News • 15 October 1997

... and later in same interview...

"All 'at we're trying to do is to
clean up the past..."

"The cynics may be able to point to the past
but we live in the future — *and we work for*
the future."

Fianna Fáil Ard-Fheis 1998

MAYBE... MAYBE NOT...

"It's a matter that an awful lot of people want or maybe an awful lot of people don't want and the people will decide ultimately."

(on Divorce)

Kenny Live • RTÉ • 17 November 1994

"People setting deadlines is always difficult... I'd rather not tie myself to an exact week or date."

(on Abortion)

Irish Examiner • 22 January 2000

NEVER!

"Although it was widespread practice in the community at that time and indeed up to today, pre-signing such cheques perhaps creates difficulties."

(on his Flood Tribunal evidence)

The Irish Times • 21 July 1999

SPLITTING HAIRS

"If hindsight were foresight, there wouldn't be a problem..."

(on his Moriarty Tribunal evidence)

The Irish Times • 30 June 2000

A TRUE DEMOCRAT

"It is no good in politics devising policies that do not have the support of the people and cannot win the support of the people."

The Irish Times • 13 May 1997

PASS THE WAFFLES

"You're a waffler, a waffler – and you've always been a waffler."

(in Dáil confrontation with Gay Mitchell)

Quoted in
Bertie Ahern — Taoiseach and Peacemaker

SO *THAT'S* WHAT THEY DO!

*"One thing that she did very successfully...
she kept in touch with all the people in the
country. She spent six months going around...
and I would hope that in her seven years,
that she keeps that up because
I think it is important."*

(on Mary Robinson's election)

Questions and Answers • RTÉ • 12 November 1990

HI, MY NAME IS...

"Well ministers... regularly — and this is a good thing in this democracy — meet people. It is a very good idea, I think, for ministers to meet people."

Prime Time • RTÉ • 26 January 1999

Bertie-isms
and
Haughey

WISHFUL THINKING

"I'd love to see Haughey get an overall majority; it's about the only thing that he hasn't achieved. I think if he got that, within a few years he would go."

In Dublin • 10 April 1991

STAND BY YER MAN

"I have been a supporter of Mr Haughey for as long as I have been in politics... I think he has been an excellent leader of this country – some people might disagree – and they're quite entitled to disagree — and he has said in his judgment when he feels it's time to go that he'll go...and I think he will go."

Questions and Answers • RTÉ • 21 October 1991

EXCELLENT MISJUDGMENT

"His judgment on the vast majority of issues has been excellent."

Questions and Answers • RTÉ • 21 October 1991

MIND YER HEAD!

"Personally, of course, I do not want to see any more fall on the head of Charlie Haughey. He's a good man who served the country well and I think he's taken a lot of knocks and he is getting older."

The Irish Times • 5 January 1998

SPLIT PERSONALITY

"You had to put your personality to one side and say that there were things he did that were not correct."

The Irish Sun • 14 May 2001

AND THE
DIFFERENCE IS...?

"I did not distance myself from him. I distanced myself from what I believe are unacceptable practices."

The Irish Times • 13 May 1997

COMMITTED
FENCE-SITTING

"I gave equal credit and equal blame to Charles Haughey's role and I stand over those things."

Later with O'Leary • RTÉ • 31 May 2000

YER HISTORY, PAL!

"I think Charlie Haughey is basically a very good man and unfortunately he got into things like the lifestyle. And the bills around the lifestyle required him to do some things that I feel very strongly about. But I actually think history will be kind to him."

The Irish Sun • 14 May 2001

The Ahern Years 1

BEFORE BERTIE	AFTER BERTIE
CJH	CJD
FLAT CAP	FLAT SCREEN
PRO-LIFE	WESTLIFE
EASI-SINGLES	MOZZARELLA
HORSLIPS	COLLAGEN IMPLANTS

What he Said...
Rough Translations

WHAT HE SAID

"I, however, am a Dubliner who was born on a farm. My father was the farm manager at All Hallowes College in Dublin. I understand and respect farming as a way of life."

The Irish Times • 19 May 1997

ROUGH TRANSLATION

I love culchies – just give me yer bleedin' vote!

WHAT HE SAID

*"(I understand) the problems of people –
people in factories and on farms, in small
businesses, at home, in schools and
communities."*

The Irish Times • 5 June 1997

ROUGH TRANSLATION

*I love everyone – just give me
yer bleedin' vote!*

WHAT HE SAID

"Nobody in this country is too rich, too powerful or too important to escape detection and investigation."

(on Tax Dodgers)

The Irish Times • 5 January 1998

ROUGH TRANSLATION

...And when we find them, we'll give them another amnesty.

WHAT HE SAID

"I would have stronger views than most people."

Evening Herald • 5 May 1998

ROUGH TRANSLATION

...I just don't know what they are...

WHAT HE SAID

"I think it is good that we have a debate on the issue. We have stuck with our system for a long time. Perhaps following the debate, we will end up with exactly the same system."

(on Electoral Reform)

The Irish Times • 20 October 1999

ROUGH TRANSLATION

*Go ahead and have your debate...
I'll do as I please anyway.*

WHAT HE SAID

"If it was Fianna Fáil on their own, I'd be happy. If it's Fianna Fáil and the PDs, I'll be happy. And if it's Fianna Fáil, the PDs and the Independents, I'll be happy. I'll work with what the people decide. Any of those will be better than losing."

The Irish Sun • 14 May 2001

ROUGH TRANSLATION

I'd go into power with anyone!

WHAT HE SAID

"I want to see the party getting down to the problems of family law and other social policy... the accountability of public funds and ensuring that the State's money is properly spent..."

Sunday Press • 24 February 1983

ROUGH TRANSLATION

You mean we'll actually have to do something?

WHAT HE SAID

"One of the great things Haughey has is that he knows so many things. On the Cabinet table, that really comes across."

In Dublin • 10 April 1991

ROUGH TRANSLATION

Haughey knows everything... except, of course, where his money comes from.

WHAT HE SAID

"All of us, including Fianna Fáil, have found ourselves in politically embarrassing situations or controversies, from which lessons have had to be learned."

The Irish Times • 4 June 1998

ROUGH TRANSLATION

Just don't get caught!

WHAT HE SAID

"... Just a way that things went on that was not an acceptable way — they maybe strictly weren't illegal but that was stretching the law... We brought in an enormous amount of laws and legislation. But things are different now — and I think we've cleaned up politics."

The Late Late Show • RTÉ • 25 May 2001

ROUGH TRANSLATION

We can't get away with it anymore... so we've been forced to clean up politics...

WHAT HE SAID

"*I won an essay competition when I was 13, on the title 'When I'll be Taoiseach'. I don't know if that was an ambition or what it was. I don't think I have that ambition now.*"

Evening Herald • 2 November 1989

ROUGH TRANSLATION

I want to be Taoiseach!

WHAT HE SAID

"I had a huge interest in the Paris riots in '68 and Ché Guevara and the Chilean revolution, you name it. But once I got interested in Fianna Fáil, I stuck with it and kept working away."

Evening Herald • 2 November 1989

ROUGH TRANSLATION

I'm boring... I'm an accountant... but I have to make myself sound interesting.

WHAT HE SAID

"Sports Campus Ireland... is a part of that vision. It's a small part in one way, and a huge part in another."

The Irish Times • 27 January 2000

ROUGH TRANSLATION

It's trivial compared to hospital waiting lists, but it will be a huge part of our spending.

WHAT HE SAID

"I made Fianna Fáil's position very clear at the Ard-Fheis. Nobody could read any ambiguous signs into it."

(on Haughey)

The Irish Times • 13 May 1997

ROUGH TRANSLATION

I hope nobody has a clue what I'm talking about...

WHAT HE SAID

"We must stop listening to the do-gooders who have all the excuses and all the problems."

The Irish Times • 7 March 1995

ROUGH TRANSLATION

We'll have to listen to Charlie McCreevy instead.

WHAT HE SAID

"If getting there means selling your soul a little bit, there isn't a profession in the world where you don't have to change your principles."

The Irish Times • 21 November 1994

ROUGH TRANSLATION

Principles? What principles?

Just What the Hell is He Talking About?

"It is as complicated or as simple as that, whatever way you want to put it. If you look at the complications, they are horrendous. Potentially, you could have trouble here, there and everywhere."

The Irish Times • 22 January 1999

What's he talking about:

(A) Failing the Leaving Cert
(B) Being Taoiseach
(C) The Middle East
(D) Making a Decision

Answer (C)

> *"It's about getting the business done, obtaining the right results. It's not about the preaching to the converted, but convincing the unpersuaded. It's not about telling them what to do, but leading them to see themselves what needs to be done, if necessary, in their own time."*

Sunday Independent • 31 December 2000

What's he talking about:

(A) Teaching
(B) Training Junior Footballers
(C) Effective Political Leadership
(D) Pulling the Perfect Pint

Answer (C)

"We prepared the ground and cut the grass for them. Some of their stuff just sticks in my gullet."

Sunday Tribune • 19 November 1989

What's he talking about:

(A) Junior Soccer Opponents
(B) The Local Chipper
(C) Farmers
(D) Employers

Answer (D)

"It is our belief that the whole matter can be dealt with in three months."

RTÉ News • 3 September 1997

What's he talking about:

(A) Decommissioning
(B) The Planning Tribunal
(C) My Wardrobe
(D) Deciding What to Have for Breakfast

Answer (B)

The Ahern Years 2

BEFORE BERTIE	AFTER BERTIE
HAIR-SHIRT	*CHARVET SHIRT*
ROCK BAND	*BOY BAND*
TERRY KEANE	*ROY KEANE*
DRUMCONDRA	*DRUMCONDRA*
BEGGING BOWL	*BERTIE BOWL*

Bertie's Inner Self

LOVE

*"I hate nobody and am never angry
at people for long.
Life's too short."*

The Irish Sun • 14 May 2001

MATERIAL THINGS

"The only things I always have in my wallet are the St Francis Xavier Novena of Grace Prayer and Programme... and the Man. United fixtures list."

Evening Herald • 5 May 1998

HAPPINESS

"When people are happy, I'm happy."

The Late Late Show • RTÉ • 25 May 2001

NIRVANA

"If I have enough to go to a match and have a few pints and a holiday and get over to United a few times a year and a few race meetings, I'm happy."

The Irish Sun • 14 May 2001

STRESS

"I just like to be straight. Otherwise it gets to me. And if something gets to me inside, then I can't operate."

Evening Herald • 5 May 1998

NEGATIVITY

"...Type of Creeping Jesus..."

"For Christ sakes, let us not get carried away by all the negative talk."

Irish Independent • 8 April 2000

The Ahern Years 3

BEFORE BERTIE	AFTER BERTIE
P&T	IT
LADA	PRADA
EARLY HOUSE	PENTHOUSE
MEDICAL CARD	GOLD CARD
STRIKES	STRIKES

The World According to Celia

DON'T FORGET, NOW!

"Sleep every night. Nothing will make you more irritable than lack of sleep."

Irish Mirror • 20 December 2000

LOITERING WITH INTENT

"In the weeks... or days before the interview, go and have a look at what the other employees and your (hopefully future) employer wear to work. Watch them going into the workplace in the morning or leaving at lunchtime."

Irish Mirror • 14 June 2000

I WISH I'D LOOKED AFTER ME FEET

"The Christmas Party season, particularly after-work drinks parties, means lots of standing around. So take care of your feet by giving yourself a foot massage."

Irish Mirror • 20 December 2000

WALKING THE WALK...

"Why not try a walk in the fresh air? Walking is free and if you walk at a reasonably fast pace, you will burn off calories, stimulate your circulation and build up your stamina."

Irish Mirror • 12 July 2000

A GOOD INVESTMENT

"If you meet people outdoors, then spend money on your overcoat."

Irish Mirror • 31 May 2000

IT'S HARDER THAN YOU THINK

"Discipline, control and balance are the keys to good shopping, and good shopping is an acquired skill."

Irish Mirror • 31 May 2000

POETRY IN MOTION

"... And what about those long skirts with the split up the back?... Well, the skirt divides at the back and catches between your legs at the front, exposing cellulite and flab on the inner thigh... So always check the view from behind, not just when standing still but when you are in motion."

Irish Mirror • 26 April 2001

The Ahern Years 4

BEFORE BERTIE	AFTER BERTIE
UNITED IRELAND	MAN UNITED
BRYLCREEM	WAX
MOBILE HOME	MOBILE PHONE
COMMIES	DOT COM
FORD CORTINA	BMW-7 SERIES

DIY BERTIE
SPEECH-MAKING 1

*WORDS NEEDED FOR A
TYPICAL BERTIE SPEECH*

People
Electorate
Statistics ("Satistics")
Criticism ("Crisicism")
Things ("Tings")
Growth ("Growt")
Citizens ("Sitisens")
Join ("Jain")
Doing ("Doin")
Competitiveness ("Competi-ness")

DIY BERTIE SPEECH-MAKING 2

PHRASES NEEDED FOR A TYPICAL BERTIE SPEECH

"I have no difficulty..."
"In the national interest..."
"My own personal opinion is irrelevant."
"At the end of the day..."
"Bring the parties together..."
"Deal with the issues..."
"I have great respect..."
"It's up to them."
"It will be dealt with in time."
"Terms of reference..."

Other Famous Berties

BERTIE THE BEET

A sugar beet called Bertie has his own cult website. The beet was originally a footnote in a weekly Internet bulletin for British Beet-growers – but Bertie's progress from a seedling to a 20-inch plant attracted fans worldwide. A website www.bertiethebeet.co.uk was set up. Unfortunately, Bertie the Beet was dug up for sugar in October 2001.

BERTIE THE BUS

Bertie the Bus is a friend of the children's animated cartoon character, Thomas the Tank Engine. Bertie's strongest characteristics are his friendly grin and his readiness to help any engine prepared to admit that – just sometimes – roads have their uses as well as rails.